Listen Up!

Listen Up!

◆

The Silence that Sells

A book to turn the self-help world on its ear

Lou Garcia and Norm Merritt

iUniverse, Inc.
New York Lincoln Shanghai

Listen Up!
The Silence that Sells

All Rights Reserved © 2003 by Norman David Merritt

No part of this book may be reproduced or transmitted in any form or by any means, graphic, electronic, or mechanical, including photocopying, recording, taping, or by any information storage retrieval system, without the written permission of the publisher.

iUniverse, Inc.

For information address:
iUniverse, Inc.
2021 Pine Lake Road, Suite 100
Lincoln, NE 68512
www.iuniverse.com

ISBN: 0-595-27453-6 (pbk)
ISBN: 0-595-65678-1 (cloth)

Printed in the United States of America

Lou
To my wife Diane. Thank you for always understanding, always being patient, and especially for always listening.

Norm
To my friends who like to listen and my family who likes to talk. May we always work well together.

Contents

LISTENING—THE SCIENCE. 1

LISTENING—THE ART 4

A NOTE FROM THE AUTHOR—LOU GARCIA—MY
    CHINESE LESSON 7

MEET JOE. 13

ONE FOR ALL 16
    A Note on Believing—Norm Merritt 17
    Joe Visits the Doctor. 18

APPREHENSIVE, PENSIVE, AND DEFENSIVE 23

THE WAY OF THE WILD. 28
    The Kitchen Table 31

THE EXACT SOLUTION?. 34

FROM THE INSIDE OUT. 36

HEARING. 37

HOLDING 39
    Modus Operandi. 44
    A Note on Technique—Norm Merritt 45
    A Note on Motives—Lou Garcia 46

HELPING 58
    Watch Body Language 58
    Help Communication. 59

Improving Your Ability To Help.................................... 61
WRAP UP.. 63

LISTENING—THE SCIENCE

> *When I am getting ready to reason with a man, I spend one-third of my time thinking about myself and what I am going to say and two-thirds about him and what he is going to say.*
>
> —Abraham Lincoln—1809-1865—16th President of the United States

Listening. What exactly is it, and why would anyone write a book about it? If we are fortunate, we're born with the ability to hear as one of our five senses. Sense of touch. Sense of taste. Sense of sight. Sense of smell. And sense of hearing. These are all second nature to us. What is there to understand about hearing? Unless we have some physical malady, we all hear things every day. Some of us may have a little trouble hearing. Some of us hear things that aren't there. And some of us only hear what we want to hear. It's easy.

But this isn't about hearing. If we need help hearing, we can tell people to speak up, to turn up the volume, or get hearing aids. No problem. This is about listening. So, what is listening? A basic definition is:

lis·ten (lĭs'en) *intr.v.*

1. To make the effort needed to hear something

2. To wait in suspense

3. To give close attention with the purpose of hearing; to give ear; to hearken; to attend.

To make the effort…To pay attention…With the purpose of hearing. To wait in suspense is a good one.

Hearing is a reaction. Someone or something initiates an action, which propagates a wave. The wave moves through the air until it contacts our eardrums. The vibration is registered accordingly, and we hear a sound. Easy and effortless.

How we register that sound is what is in question. It's a loud noise. It's a soft noise. Everything is noise until our brains make the effort to process the sound. The loud noise becomes a gunshot, a car backfiring, or thunder. The soft noise is the breeze through a tree in early spring, or a whisper. Listening is making the effort and taking the time to categorize and understand the sounds that surround us.

So, listening is an action. Listening is a learned behavior. Our parents tell us elevator music is a good sound and our music is noise. They're wrong of course, and we eventually learn that our music rocks. Then we have kids, and they learn for themselves that we were wrong about our music; but their music is awesome, the sound of their generation.

If we've been learning to listen from day one, why do we need a lesson in it now? Because whenever we look at communication, the most important part is to listen; otherwise, we're just talking to ourselves. The ongoing learning process for listening is little more than just a day-to-day activity that we attribute to personal growth. In school we learn how to read—the alphabet, the sounds the letters make, and how they form words. We learn how to write—the alphabet, how to use those letters to form words and those words to construct sentences. We learn how to speak—public speaking. Was anything ever worse than that feeling of getting up in front of the class for the first time and presenting a speech about your summer vacation? But did the teacher ever bring you to the front of the class to stand there in front of everyone and…listen? I would have to read Melville's *Moby Dick*. I would have to write a 500-word essay about the metaphors of the conflict between a big white whale and Captain Ahab. Then I would nervously have to make my way to the podium and give a speech based on my essay. Meanwhile, the others sat there staring out the window if they weren't rolling their eyes at the sheer boredom of it all. A few were worried that they would be called on next. But no one was listening to me. That didn't bother me. Because I knew that when I went back to my seat, I would be looking out the same windows and not paying attention to anyone. And the teacher wouldn't care. She was only interested in making us better readers, writers, and speakers.

Then we grow up and enter the working world. We want to go out and sell, sell, sell because that means we can make money, money, money. We want to say things to make money. We want to do things to make money. When we need advice, we always ask for advice on "What can I say?" "What can I do to make it happen?" And there are our roles in personal relationships to consider. In both personal and professional situations, we want to do more, have more, and be more. We may evaluate our results and relationships and discover there may indeed be a need to improve our effectiveness in these roles. To have a better life, we choose to do better and to be better. A key area of focus is often in the field of communication. We can be better salespeople, managers, leaders, parents, friends, and neighbors if we can communicate more effectively. Our performance will improve and our relationships thrive. In our efforts to make things right, we rush out to buy a book to find out just what it is we need to say and do to close the sale or to better the relationship. We want to learn to organize content, deliver our message, and develop the necessary techniques. These actions are all directed outwards. We want to say and do things to influence others. We want to say and do things to make the world a better place. We want to say and do things to make others better. We want to say and do things. The more we can say, the more we can do, and the better everyone else will be. Say…do. Say…do. Say…These books we read, these lessons we learn can help, but perhaps the most important part of effective communication is not what we say, or even how we say it, but rather our ability and willingness to listen to others.

The greatest extent of training we get on listening is when the teacher says, "OK, children…listen up." So we have to teach ourselves. But at such a young age, we are students of life, not teachers. If we learn to listen wrong, we form bad habits and improper techniques. The purpose of this book is to help you understand the responsibilities of listening and the expectations the speaker will place on you. The purpose of this book is to slow you down, to shut you up…temporarily. The purpose is to stop you for a moment so that you can learn how to listen. Once you know how to listen, you'll know even better what to say, and you'll be able to make the world a better place whether it's by bringing happiness to someone, by swaying someone's opinion, or by closing a sale.

LISTENING—THE ART

∘ ∘
The less you talk, the more you're listened to.
—*Abigail van Buren—American Advice Columnist—"Dear Abby"*

Communication is a two-way street. In order for there to be communication, someone must speak, and someone must listen. Unfortunately, when we communicate, there is a percentage of people who don't listen. It's easy to tell when someone is speaking. That part is obvious. The doubt creeps in when the party of the first part feels like the party of the second part isn't participating. "No matter what I do, my children won't hear what I say." "No matter how hard I try, no one listens to me." At times, everyone has thought the person he was talking to wasn't listening.

In fact, during a conversation, the person supposedly listening is distracted by any number of things. 40% are reflecting on their past. 30% are anticipating their future. And 15% are concerned with other things. That leaves only 15% of the "listeners" actively listening, paying undivided attention. As we listen, words go…"in one ear and out the other." Practically all of us are guilty of this at some time or another.

This isn't intentional. That is part of being a social animal. We are by nature curious and head off in several directions at once. That comes from our early nature of being hunter-gatherers. It's true for anyone. We start listening to someone then begin talking to ourselves. "Yeah. I remember the one time that happened to me…" Or, "Yeah! Great idea! When I get back to my office…" Or, "Does every box of Raisin Bran have two scoops or is it only the big box? Maybe they use smaller scoops."

At that point, we've left the moment and are no longer listening. That was never the intent, but it's so easy to get sidetracked. One word inspires an unexpected train of thought that we can't keep on track. One glance at something moving out the corner of our eye, and we're off and running down another mental path.

You've all heard: "God gave us one mouth but two ears. Why? So we can listen twice as much as we talk." Or, "Take a tip from nature: You're ears aren't made to shut, but your mouth is." Any way you look at it, the ears play a prominent role in our lives and should be used accordingly.

When we communicate, we can speak an average of 135-175 words per minute. There are those who can tip those scales a bit…especially when excited. That's between two to three words a second. Give some people a little caffeine, and they can do that every second of every minute of every hour without any apparent sign or breathing or tiring. These people can wear your ears out.

Or can they? Many people will tell others to: "Slow down! You're speaking too fast." One response may be: "No, I'm not. You're listening too slow." Actually, the other person is right. The average person can hear between 400 to 500 words per minute. That means there is a lot of space between what is said and what we listen to. And that means we often hear at least twice as much as what someone says.

We are by nature eager to help others. Since we listen so fast, process the information so quickly, we know what they're going to say before they can say it. So, we try to be nice. We want to save them time. We interrupt them as a means to help them because they're just too slow. We think we understand them because we know how we would finish the same sentences. They must be thinking what we think they're thinking because we think we know everything.

The 7 Habits of Highly Effective People is a very popular book by Stephen Covey. Of those seven habits, the fifth one states that your goal should be *to first understand others then to have others understand you.* Many times, we reverse that habit because we know what is right. We know what everyone needs. "If they understand me, they would like me." "If they listen to me, they would see I am right and buy my product." "If my wife only understood me, everything would be fine." "If everyone saw things my way, the world would be a better place." It all comes down to understanding. Well, keep this in mind. Most people feel the same way you do. If you intend to make someone understand you, how do you intend to do it? Probably by talking to them. If everyone feels the same way, everyone wants to talk. The problem with this is that now, no one is listening. You don't hear them. They don't hear you.

Someone has to make the first move. Imagine taking a trip to your local mall. You and a stranger simultaneously approach the double set of glass doors at the entrance. Try telling that person: "If you open this door for me, I'll open the next door for you." WRONG! Any time you tell people to open it for you, they will think you selfish and vain. But, if you open the door for them first, they will be more likely to respond and return the favor as you approach the next door. By offering simple courtesies, you establish a rapport that nurtures the habit of giving back when given to. People want to be understood. People want to be heard, listened to.

A NOTE FROM THE AUTHOR—LOU GARCIA—MY CHINESE LESSON

One who cares is one who listens.

—*J. Richard Clarke*

I grew up a second-generation Hispanic American. My parents were born in Cuba. I grew up listening to Spanish as much as English. My job as a corporate trainer has taken me from San Juan to Seattle, from Montreal to Maui. As part of a multi-national corporation, I have had the opportunity to encounter a diverse group of individuals of many nationalities. Their language skills are equally wide-ranging. Some people speak English while others don't speak English very well. Listening takes on even more importance.

Prior to presenting this topic to a predominantly Chinese professional group, my host apologized to me. "I so sorry. My English not very good."

This was going to be a challenge. My response to her was: "That's OK. My Chinese is awful."

Throughout that first day, I got a feel for the group, and they grew a bit more accustomed to me...after I realized that even if the mind can process 400-500 words a minute, I needed to slow down since English was not their first language and since they needed time to translate in order to understand.

During one of our breaks, my host showed me the Chinese symbol for "listen."

It looked a lot more complicated to me than "listen" or "escuche" (Spanish for "listen") or even several other languages I don't know:

Écoutez	(French)
Ascolti	(Italian)
Escute	(Portuguese)
Luister	(Dutch)
Hören	(German)

As with most languages, we learn to read and recognize words. We seldom take time to learn the etymology or history of a word. Look at Spanish, French, Italian, and Portuguese. They all look and sound similar because they all have a similar history. Many of those who speak Chinese are simply taught and accept that this is the symbol for "listen." They never actually look at the words. They don't take time to analyze the different components.

When my host took time to explain the symbol to me, the idea of listening took on a whole new meaning. The symbol, "**tìng**" is comprised of four components. The first part:

is taken from the symbol "**ěrduo**"

which means "Ear." OK. That's understandable. You use your ears to hear. So the rest of the symbol should just turn the noun *ear* into the verb ***listen***.

But there is more to it than that, which she made clear to be by politely raising her index finger to point out that more was to come.

The second part:

comes from the symbol "**gúowáng**"

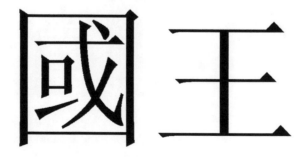

which means "king." Intriguing. This meant that when you listen, you must do it with respect. Would you interrupt the king when he is talking? Probably not. The king might say, "I decree that..." You break in with: "Well, what I think is..." No! To interrupt the king would be foolish. Would you finish his sentence? Doubtful. Let the king talk. If you cut off his sentence, he'll cut off your head. Likewise, when we listen, we should be very respectful of the speaker. We must demonstrate that we hold him in high regard. Poor listening reflects a point of view that the other person is not important. Customers, prospects, employees, and family members want to feel important. They want to know that you think they are important, that they matter to you. Listening, or the lack thereof, is the proof they need to make that decision.

So, we have ear and king. Use your ears and listen with respect. But that's only half the symbol. There's still more to go. The third part:

although somewhat harder for me to see (ironically), comes from the symbol "**yǎnjīng**"

which means "eye." Look. See. Pay attention. Show people you are listening. If you are not looking, you are not listening. It doesn't mean you need to stare at them without motion and without blinking, but be attentive. Don't allow yourself to be distracted by everything else around you. If you're not showing them that you are paying attention, then they won't think you are listening, and that makes people feel crummy.

At times, a husband and wife will end up in some conversation. While she's talking to him, he is listening intermittently, waiting for her to make her point. Well, for her, the whole conversation was her point. So, every time he reads the paper or the nutritional information on the cereal box while she's trying to have a conversation with him, he's taking away from the relationship.

So, it's listening with respect and showing that you're paying attention. Ear. King. Eye. But there's more. The final part of the symbol:

comes from "**yī xīnzàng**"

which means "one heart." When you listen, you must listen with your heart. Everyone is familiar with the term "heart-to-heart." Having a heart-to-heart talk with someone means that when one is talking, the other is listening at a higher, more intimate level. It means listening with empathy.

em·pa·thy (ĕm'pŭ-thē) *n.*

1. Identification with and understanding of another's motives, feelings, and situations.

The goal is to be empathic listeners. Empathy comes from the Greek words "Em" meaning "In" and "Pathos" meaning "Feeling." Empathy means that when someone is sharing with you, it is important to understand the feelings, not just the words. It is to really understand where they are coming from and how they feel about what they are communicating. It is moving into the other person's world. With our eyes, we demonstrate that they are important. With our hearts, we discover what is important to them.

MEET JOE

o o o o o o o o o o o o o o o o o o o o o o o o o o o o o o
Listening, not imitation, may be the sincerest form of flattery.

—Dr. Joyce Brothers—American Psychologist and Television and Radio Personality

Enter Joe Saylesmin. He is you, He is me. He's pretty much anyone and everyone, no one in particular. Picture Joe having this conversation with his wife Martha…whom he loves dearly by the way.

She said to him from across the table: "We never go out."

Joe's taken aback. He let the corner of the paper fall so that he could look into one eye. He raises his eyebrows. What word is it that he hears and focuses on? "Never!" He put down the newspaper. "Never!? Do you remember in 1982 when I took you to the ABBA concert?"

That obviously struck a nerve with Martha. "That was 1982!"

He wasn't about to let her think she was right. "Yeah! But you said never!"

"Oh, you're not *listening*."

Joe knew better. Of course he was listening. "Of course I'm listening." He proceeds to repeat every word in order to prove he could indeed listen and read the newspaper at the same time. "You said we **never** go out." He feels he won the argument. He may have won in words, but he lost in the relationship. Is it better to win or to stay married? "Now, have some pie."

He didn't know if she was getting angry or frustrated. "You don't understand."

Now, that struck a nerve with him. "Of course I understand. What are you trying to say? I'm stupid?"

"Yes!" Actually, she didn't say yes, but that's how it felt. He pretty much knew he would be sleeping on the sofa that night, and it wasn't a very comfortable sofa. Not only did he lose, she lost as well.

In that conversation, Joe was listening to the words. It's easier that way. He can fight with words. He can argue and reason with words. He was hearing with his ears. What he needed here was a little empathy. She didn't literally mean they had never gone out, but at the moment, she felt as if they never did. If he had put down the paper and focused on Martha, took time to understand her feelings behind the words, and to clarify, he might have thought before speaking and answered:

"So, what you're saying is we need to spend some more time together?"

She would calmly respond with "Exactly."

If he had heard it that way, the way she meant it, do you know what he might have said? "You're right." Now, they can make plans to bring them closer together. By being open to feelings, both are less defensive, more open, and can feel more secure in the relationship.

"I love you, Joe. Have another piece of pie."

"Cool." He got extra pie, and he got to sleep in his own bed with his wife…whom he loves dearly.

Most disagreements are not disagreements. They're misunderstandings. We listen to the words and get caught up in the text, taking all of it as one literal expression rather than bits and pieces, each with its own intent and interpretation. In a perfect world, the person speaking would say exactly what he or she means. But Joe grew up around people who always said: "I know it's what I said, but it's not what I meant." Conversation is so much more than the words. Words are only a small part of it. You need to "listen" to the body language. You need to "listen" to the emotions. In dialogue between you and someone else, you cannot control what the other person says. You only have control over your own words and actions. If you can listen with greater empathy, you should be able to read beyond the words.

Empathic listening is combining all four parts of "**tìng**."

Ear, eye, king, and heart. With your ears, you can listen to their words. With your eyes, you can listen to their body language. With your heart, you can listen to their emotions. Using your other senses to hear is very similar to synethesia.

syn·es·the·sia (sĭn'ĭs-thē'zhŭ) *n.*

1. The condition in which **one type of stimulation evokes the sensation of another**, such as when hearing a sound produces the visualization of a color.

Isn't that a little different than just: "I hear you?"

You want to focus on listening. Maintain eye contact. Show real concern in what they're doing and saying. Don't just sit there with your chin in your hand and stare at them.

Then focus on showing concern. Demonstrate it by letting them know you know. This will make them feel understood. Once they feel understood, they'll be open to understanding you.

That isn't to say that all you want is to understand…Period. As salespeople, we do have something we want to say, something we want to accomplish. You're in that conversation for a reason. In a personal relationship, you want to express yourselves, your worries, or your dreams. Even then, you're selling. You're all salespeople even if the only thing you're trying to get someone to buy is your point, your argument, or your idea. But what better way is there to stress your point, make your argument, express your idea, or close your sale than to set up the right environment for listening. Even in front of a roomful of people, when you can't necessarily listen to all the individuals…with your ears, you can still absorb the group dynamics, respect their time and presence, let them know you care, watch their actions and reactions and direct yourself accordingly.

Listening involves the ears, eyes, and heart. This is the key in relationships, sales, customer service, and leadership. People do not want to be heard; they want to be understood.

ONE FOR ALL

A person hears only what he understands.

—*Johann Wolfgang von Goethe—1749-1832—German Poet, Dramatist, and Novelist.*

For the most part, listening sounds easy. It is making an effort to hear what is said, not just letting words go in one ear and out the other. It is respecting the person to whom you are listening, actually respecting the person's time and place instead of meandering off into nowhere or somewhere else. It is watching the person, avoiding needless distractions. It is showing that you care and sincerely demonstrating that concern. How difficult is that? Some people claim that they can multi-task. Some people actually can multi-task. In truth, you may be able to multitask tasks, but you cannot multitask people. You may think: Ear. King. Eye. Heart. That's four things to do at once. Therefore, it must be possible to multi-task people, but this isn't multi-tasking. You are not performing individual tasks simultaneously. These aren't even tasks. They're all second nature. Seeing and hearing are senses. Feeling is emotional. Respecting others is usually learned early on in life. These are four components of a single task—understanding. So, if it's so simple, what is it that gets in the way of listening?

It's the small things, things that are barely perceptible to us because they are second nature as well. It's our own feelings. "Our products are good." "Our ideas are right." "We have the solutions." "We're here to help you, so shut up and listen…and have some pie." These are all feelings. As competent professionals, of course we feel good about what we do. We believe in what we do. We have to, or we wouldn't be doing it.

A Note on Believing—Norm Merritt

One thing I always hated was taking part in debates in high school English and Public Speaking classes. It was easy enough when I could choose my side. If I believed in it, I could argue the point endlessly and could usually sway an opinion or two. I had to listen to the other team's arguments so I could counter them. Later, the teacher would let us pick our sides for an argument then trick us by making us switch. That was easy enough to get around. I could pick the side I didn't want to be on, knowing I would get to make the argument I wanted. Still later, the teacher would make us pick sides—pro or con. After the teams were set, she would choose the argument. With practice, I could talk circles around the others, but my heart wasn't in an argument if I didn't agree with it. So, there were times when I simply wouldn't listen or care. I could win by out-talking the others or getting them flustered. But I didn't really win anything. For the moment, I got more points, but I never convinced anyone in the long run.

Likewise, a salesperson who doesn't believe in what he is doing or selling or who isn't truly concerned about the customer can double-talk a customer into a purchase he doesn't really need. It works for the short-term, but then the customer later has time to think and changes his mind. The salesperson loses the sale and the customer. A professional needs to determine who needs the service or product. For multiple products or services, the salesperson must determine which product or service is best suited for the customer. To do this, you must create an environment that prepares the other person for listening and learning.

As Helen Keller said: *Any teacher can take a child to the classroom, but not every teacher can make him learn.* This sounds like: you can lead a horse to water, but you can't make him drink. It's the same principle. The teacher has to sell knowledge to the student. The teacher has to convince the student of the importance and value of learning. How does the teacher do this? He or she must establish the environment, show concern, find the student's needs. How is this done? It is done by finding the motivation zone for the student. The teacher can't tell the student that every astronaut needs to be good at math and expect the student to excel when the student wants to be a chef. Instead of all physics and calculus, math becomes splitting and doubling recipes.

Creating that motivation zone around the student will encourage the student to learn. Creating the motivation zone around the prospective recruit will encourage him to join. Creating the motivation zone around the client will encourage her to purchase your product or service. This zone is created in part by listening.

When you were driving to work this morning, you were listening to the same radio station as everyone else—WII-FM. East or west of the Mississippi, WII-FM. Whether you were driving, flying, or pedaling your bike—WII-FM. If you were watching television, even if you don't have a radio, you were listening to WII-FM. What station is that? It's the *What's In It For Me* station.

What we really need to do is find out: What's in it for THEM? What are THEIR wants? What are THEIR needs? If you don't take time to discover their needs, you will most likely not meet their needs. What happens then?

Joe Visits the Doctor

Joe Saylesmin doesn't really like going to a doctor. He sees the white coat…his pulse races, his blood pressure goes up, and he starts to get cold and sweaty. That'll show symptoms he's not even there for. With a wife and two kids, sometimes he has to go to make sure he can stay healthy for them.

The doctor walks in with Joe's blue patient folder and looks at him from across the examining room. Joe stutters, "You know, doc. My throat's a little sore. My wife has a cold. My kids are sick…"

The doctor's tiny little cell phone that Joe didn't even notice before rings. "Could you hold on a moment? I'll be right back." He puts down the folder and leaves the room. Joe sits there twiddling his thumbs then bends down to tie his shoe which he had somehow caught on the corner of the bed.

Just as he pulls tight on the strings, the doctor comes back in. "You were saying something about your foot…"

"Throat!" Joe quickly corrected him. "It's my throat. We're all sick at home…"

The nurse comes to the door and pulls the doctor aside. The doctor says, "Excuse me. I really need to take care of this."

Needless to say, Joe's a little frustrated by this and nervous. He grabs the *Good Housekeeping* magazine from the counter beside him and fans his armpits. He expected the doctor would try to do a throat culture. Joe imagined him ramming that huge cotton swab down his throat, scraping his tonsils. If he didn't throw up, the doctor would probably pull out some blackberry seeds from the pie his wife had made the night before. Or…heaven forbid…what if he wanted to give Joe a shot? His fear of needles was worse than his fear of doctors.

Finally, the doctor came back in looking a little distracted, carrying a green folder. "OK, we'll schedule surgery for a week from Thursday."

"Surge…" Joe went flush and felt the room spinning.
"Nurse! We could use some ice in here…"

What would you do if this happened to you? You'd probably run and never look back. What do you call a doctor like that? You call him a quack. In legal terms, it's malpractice.

> **mal·prac·tice** (măl-prăk'tĭs) *n.*
>
> 1. Improper or negligent treatment of a patient, by a physician, resulting in loss, injury, or damage.
>
> **2. The act or an instance of improper practice.**
>
> 3. Improper or unethical conduct by someone holding a professional or official position.

If a doctor prescribes medication or treatment without first diagnosing the problem, that's malpractice.

We want our doctors to be competent in their practice. We don't want to be their "practice." We want them to be professionals so we can trust their advice. In whatever role we are playing, there are people who expect us to perform our best. They count on our knowledge and experience. They count on our ability to understand them and their unique situations. A client wants a salesperson to understand his needs or the needs of his organization. He expects professionalism and competence. Listening reflects both. If we think of the occasions when we are the customers, we know that we expect the same from others.

We also want doctors with a good "bedside manner." That is that we want them to be knowledgeable about medicine, yet also be willing and able to relate to us a people, not just case studies.

What about as a salesperson? It's fundamentally the same thing. Your actions may not carry the same weight as medical malpractice, and you may not end up killing or maiming someone, but as a professional, you have an ethical responsibility to diagnose before you prescribe.

We cannot impress others with our skills if we have not previously demonstrated a concern for them and their situation. If you go into a store to buy a new suit, you want a salesperson to know suits, to know styles, to know fabrics, to know fitting, and, more importantly, to know you. The only way for that salesperson to know you is to listen, and when appropriate, ask questions to help identify your needs. When buying a new home, you want the real estate agent to know houses, architecture, construction, and the neighborhood, but you also want him to know that you love trees, have two beautiful children, and hate traffic.

The best performers in every industry know that listening demonstrates both professionalism and trustworthiness. You cannot have one without the other and expect to be successful. No one wants to be sold; they want to buy. And they want to buy from people they can trust. Trust is built by active listening.

Take the financial services industry for example (Coincidentally, this is Joe's occupation.). So many people think insurance salespeople are quacks all because a certain few in the past may have been less than ethical. Suppose as a new financial-services professional, Joe runs out gung ho after being trained on a product. He approaches three different prospective clients.

"You, buy term; invest the difference." *(That's term life insurance.)*

"You, buy term; invest the difference."

"You, buy term; invest the difference."

"Buy term; invest the difference for EVERYBODY!"

Can anyone expect to get excited about this? No! Why? Because no one solution is right for everybody. Even if it is right, they may not believe you.

Across town, Anita, Joe's neighbor and an agent for a different company, has garnered a little more experience and a little more training on another product. She approaches three prospective clients from her cold-call list.

"Hi, I'm Anita. You, buy VUL!" *(That's Variable Universal Life Insurance.)*

"Hello, my name is Ms. Bydis. You, buy VUL!"

"You, buy VUL!"

"VUL for EVERYBODY!"

Is that better? No. Even if it is a great solution, Anita didn't take the time to diagnose the situation; therefore, she cannot justifiably recommend or prescribe the solution.

Still, elsewhere in the same town, Joe's friend Bart has been with his multi-level marketing company for some time now, and after learning from his mistakes, he's done pretty well for himself. He lost some clients early on, but he has had pretty good retention with most. He sees it as a great opportunity for everyone. After the last check he received, he got really excited.

Bart went running through the streets. "You, join my company!"

"You, join my company. Be a success like me."

"You! I don't know you, but you need this most of all. Join my company."

"EVERYONE! JOIN MY COMPANY! IT'S RIGHT FOR YOU!" And he skips away. Bart might be completely right, but if those people don't feel understood, if they don't understand why the opportunity is right for them, it won't work.

"With my company, you can get a car!" She and her husband already have two cars. She doesn't need another one.

"With my company, you can send your kids to college!" But they don't have kids. They had been trying hard because they wanted children more than anything, but the doctors told them they couldn't. Ouch!

With so many wrong things that a person can say, where can we find a script that tells us what we should say? We determine what we need to say by first determining the client's needs. To determine the client's needs, we have to listen to the client. The best script for listening…begins as a blank page.

"You know, it's this job…"

"My company! It's for you." Hold on! That's not in the script. Don't jump in. You haven't identified the problem. Identifying the problem requires asking and listening. Your script is written based on what the other person says and is subject to change without notice.

The morning after Joe ran off gung ho trying to sell his new product to everyone, he returned to work. On the elevator, he ran into his acquaintance Miss Treetid. There was no one else in the elevator with them. "You know, Joe…It's this job." That's all she said, expecting Joe to rush into one of his tirades.

Joe chimed in when he realized the chance here. "My company…" He stopped himself. "What is it about your job?"

Miss Treetid would have stepped back, impressed by this show of concern, but she was already leaning against the elevator. "It's going nowhere. They don't treat me well."

"How long have you felt this way?"

"A while."

"Why haven't you done something about it?"

"The job market's not that great right now."

All this time, Joe is gathering information, setting up an environment conducive for understanding. "Besides that, is there anything else bothering you?"

"Yeah. They haven't given me a raise in a year."

"Is that a problem?"

"Sure it is. I've run myself ragged for them."

"Do you think you'll you get one next year?"

"Probably not…" The elevator reached her floor, and the door opened.

"Maybe we can talk more about this later."

"Maybe," she said with a smile.

If we take a moment to listen rather than jumping in with both feet, we stand a better chance of not stepping on someone else's toes. If we don't ask questions, and instead rush to a solution, they could get scared. It's like feeding pigeons in the park. If we take a seat and gently scatter the breadcrumbs around, they come close and take time to eat, comfortable with your presence. But if you run through the flock and throw the crumbs, they scatter, frightened by your excitement.

APPREHENSIVE, PENSIVE, AND DEFENSIVE

○ ○
No one ever listened himself out of a sale.

—Lou Garcia

Fear is brought to you courtesy of the amygdala.

Amygdala n:

The almond-shaped neural structure in the anterior part of the temporal lobe of the cerebrum connected with the hypothalamus and the hippocampus and the cingulate gyrus; as part of the limbic system **it plays an important role in motivation and emotional behavior**

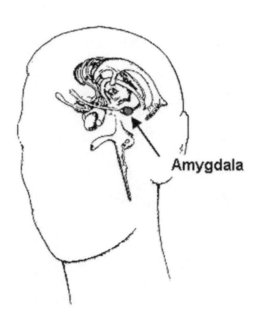

The amygdala controls and inspires our response to danger. This is generally broken down into fight (a mother bear protecting her cubs), flight (a gazelle trying to outrun the pursuing lion), and freeze (a deer in the headlights of an oncoming semi). Think back to times when you were frightened. Can you come up with any other responses? These are the fundamental reactions to any dangerous situation.

When we rush an unsuspecting prospective client, the client gets apprehensive. When we unwittingly accost friends or strangers with our point, they get pensive. When we are quick to disagree with people, they get defensive. It happens to practically everyone sooner or later because of our instincts.

Even extremely confident Joe can be caught off guard. He worked late that day scheduling appointments including one made with Miss Treetid. Some of the lights were off in the nearly empty parking deck. He had to walk through the shadows to his car. From the corner of his eye, he sees something rushing towards him. In the near darkness, he can't make it out clearly. His amygdala grabs at him from inside. It becomes a little nervous and speaks to him. "Beware." But neither Joe nor his amygdala know what to do yet—fight, flight, or freeze.

Freezing is a pretty good choice. A Tyrannosaurus Rex doesn't have good eyesight and relies on motion to find its prey. Joe's hair stands up on end. Why? Look at cats. It makes them look bigger. His heart pumps harder, sending adrenaline coursing through his veins. Nature is preparing him for fight or flight. Either way, he would need adrenaline for extra strength and speed.

The amygdala signals for his cortisone levels to increase to thicken his blood. Thicker blood would help slow the bleeding. Lions and tigers and bears…Oh my!

There are then a number of other reactions to the alarm. Blood pressure rises to increase capacity. As blood is pulled away from the stomach, the stomach becomes more acidic, a strong signal that something is up. This results in the "gut instinct" with which we are familiar. Sugars and fats are released to fuel and drive performance. Our senses become heightened. All of this is automatic. It is our response to fear, fear of the unknown, and fear of what we know to be harmful. It is our fear of being sold, of being rejected, of being hurt.

As the enemy comes closer, it becomes obvious to Joe that it's a person. "OK, so it's not a dinosaur." He can possibly defend himself. Joe puts his keys between his fingers so he can stab his assailant's eyes out. The amygdala has decided to stay and fight rather than run. There was Joe's pride to consider after all.

A couple of yards closer, Joe realizes it's his friend Bart. He hesitates before putting the keys away as he tries to remember if Bart owes him any money. "No, he paid me Monday." The amygdala relaxes. Joe had forgotten about the weekly handball match he had with Bart.

Everything returns to normal once he realizes he isn't in any danger.

The amygdala serves us very well when there are dangers out there. In the "Wizard of Oz" when Dorothy was in the dark forest along the yellow brick road, the amygdala kept her moving cautiously through her fear of wild beasts because she had nothing there to protect her but the Scarecrow, the Tin Man, and a tiny little Toto. *Lions and tigers and bears…Oh my!* Today, our contact with scary beasts is more limited. Where can we find the scary lions? How about the zoo? Does your amygdala go crazy? No. The tigers are sleeping. The lions are confined to their cages. The bears can be found in the wild, but there is a lot less wild to find.

But are there scary things out there that do cause the amygdala to set off the alarms?

Life Insurance Sales…Oh my!

Multi-level marketing meetings…Oh my!

Sales! Sales! Sales…Oh my!

Life Insurance, sales, recruiting, multi-level, team building, business opportunities, the knock on the door, or the ringing phone at dinnertime. All of these things are scary. They all cause people concern. For those people in sales, for those who are extremely passionate about what they do, these things don't scare them because it's what they do: it's who they are. But we have to be aware of others because if we rush towards them, they get scared just like Bambi in headlights.

When that doctor called for surgery, Joe got scared. Right or wrong, he wasn't comfortable with that decision. Did the doctor plan on operating on Joe's throat or his foot?

Whenever we take advice from a professional, there is a factor called trust.

trust (trŭst) *n.*

Strong reliance on the ability, integrity, or character of a person or object.

Integrity and character are reasonably similar. Trust is, therefore, two-fold, comprised of character and competence. How would Joe be able to build trust with that doctor? And how could the doctor get Joe to trust him? The doctor needed to listen to Joe. He needed to take time to diagnose the illness before prescribing the solution. And Joe had to be willing to communicate with the doctor. Of course the doctor made him nervous, but the more Joe could communicate with him and describe his symptoms and feelings…and exactly what was hurting—his throat not his foot—the more understood he would feel.

A person's feelings are very important when it comes to taking advice. Did you ever have advice you didn't take? Or do you know someone who didn't take advice that was given to him? Why didn't you take that advice?

The person giving the advice might have been competent, but you weren't necessarily sure of his character. Or the advisor might have had a great character, but you weren't sure of his competence. Maybe you thought you knew better.

When many people start out in a new company and are on the beginning of the learning curve, having limited experience with the products they are offering, potential customers might trust their character, but not their competence. When Joe first started with his company, he approached friends that he had known for some time. They knew Joe was a good and honest man with nothing but the best intentions, but they questioned how much he knew about this new job he had started when he previously worked in an entirely different industry.

But Joe learned as he went by taking someone more experienced with him on his early appointments. It is possible to borrow someone else's credibility and competence when others trust you and have confidence in your character.

Character is a little different. If someone trusts you, you can loan out some confidence in someone else. "I trust him 100%." If they trust you and think you are a good judge of character, they will be willing to give your associate a chance. Unlike competence—"He's worked in the industry for 12 years."—which means he must be knowledgeable about what he is doing, character is more personal and based on the customer's familiarity and past experiences. Character is demonstrated by how well you walk the walk and talk the talk. It shows that you know what you're doing. Ask yourself if your competence shows. You must have confidence in your competence if you want someone to have confidence in you. But it doesn't mean that you know everything about what you do or that you immediately have all the answers. Even if you do have the answers, you had better hear the questions first.

Character is equally important in most situations. When Joe wanted to buy a digital camcorder, he didn't know the sales associate, but he had bought from the store previously and had not had problems with his purchases. So, he felt confident that the associate would know what he was doing. Joe was confident in the company because of his history with it. That lasted only as long as it took the associate to lead Joe right to the most expensive items they carried as soon as Joe asked for a digital camcorder.

"If you want a camcorder, this is the one you need." The associate was clearly trying to make the sale that would give him the best commission.

Character in the individual wasn't initially important to Joe, but Joe quickly backed away. As someone once said: *People don't care what you know until they know that you care.* This is the basis of the listening model. Rushing in sets fear in motion. As soon as you say, "Everyone needs what I have," the amygdala kicks in. But your silence is very soothing to someone's amygdala, especially when combined with listening.

THE WAY OF THE WILD

Opportunities are often missed because we are broadcasting when we should be receiving.

—*Unknown*

You justify your actions because you are rushing for a reason. Everyone knows what a stoplight is. Some people don't pay attention to them, but everyone is familiar with them. For those of you not lucky enough to work at home, this morning when you were listening to WII-FM while driving to the office, you came up on a red light. That meant stop. So, you stopped.

The next light was red. So you stopped.

The next was red. So you stopped but were a little perturbed because you were suddenly running late.

The next light was a couple of miles away. You rushed up to it. Fortunately, it was green. Green means go, so you kept going.

The next light…red.

The next…red.

The next light turned yellow as you approached it, so you sped up. You gunned the car to get through the intersection because yellow means…*Go really fast!*

No! Yellow means slow down. Prepare to stop. If you can't make it through while driving at or slower than the posted speed limit, you need to stop, not speed up. But what do most of us do when we see yellow? We mash the accelerator, and we speed up to make it through.

There tends to be one very distinct problem with this. Someone else has somewhere to be as well. If you're running late, there's a good possibility he is too. And that someone happens to be across the way at the same intersection and is trying to turn. He sees the light change from green to yellow too. He speeds up to make the turn because he was listening to the same station WII-FM. He had to get to work and would only fall farther behind if he missed the light.

Suddenly, there are two 6000-pound vehicles speeding up, coming in different directions and approaching the same point. Is there a problem?

CRASH! Yes, there is most definitely a problem.

It's the same with communication. When we speed up to make our point or close the deal, we may have a collision.

Joe's friend, neighbor, and racquetball partner Bart used to have way too many wrecks working in his Multi-Level-Marketing company. Joe, Bart, and, another friend Hank met for lunch one day. Hank commented, "I ain't got no money."

Bart quickly responded, "Really? Join my company! It's only $200 to start, and $300 for the initial supplies."

Hank looked at Bart with raised eyebrows. "You're not listening. I said I have no money."

Bart's response was, "Of course I'm listening. You can get more money with my company."

Joe wanted to tell Bart what he was doing wrong but didn't want to interfere by giving unsolicited advice.

Could Bart have the right solution? It's possible that it would work in the long term, but Hank had a short-term issue to consider. Bart needed to read the signals properly.

Another time, Bart was at Joe's for a party and was listening to Joe's cousin Anita speaking with her half-sister. Anita said, "I just don't have any time to do the things I want to do. Tuesday nights are the only time I have free anymore."

Bart interrupted. "Really? Try my company! We have meetings every Tuesday. On Saturdays, we have training sessions to help you learn faster. It just takes a little extra time for a while."

Anita shook her head. She had met Bart before and knew how he could be. "I said I don't have any time. You're not listening."

"Of course I'm listening," Bart retorted. "You need more time. You can get more time by joining us." Once again, Bart needed to read the signals properly because it might be good eventually, but maybe not now or maybe not the way he had in mind.

Why do we rush through everything? We rush to get where we're going. We want to push our company. We want to sell our product. We want to make our point. If we slow down, we might miss the opportunity.

But if we don't slow down, we might miss the opportunity. If we speed through the intersection, we might run into some 6000-pound problems, and we may be the ones to blame. Welcome to the wonderful word of sales. Whether you're selling yourself, your ideas, your products, or your opportunities, people will blame you when things go awry. People will tend to make you the root of all evil.

Take Joe's company for instance. "Financial services..." Joe rationalizes. "At least it's not the world's oldest profession." Maybe. But one of the first banks was started by members of the world's oldest profession. So that makes financial services the world's second oldest profession and is commonly confused with the first. People have come to believe it's all about the money. Selling is all about the money. That is how most customers feel because it's the way they have been taught and treated. It's this way because so many times, no one has taken the time to understand them.

What do clients think about salespeople?
"They're pushy."
What do salespeople think about clients?
"They're slow and stupid." Joe says, "I'm pushy because you're slow. I'm trying to help you finish your sentence."

Clients think: "Leave me alone. Why can't they take no for an answer?"
Salespeople think: "Clients always have excuses. They're babies. They don't know what they need."

Clients think: "You don't care what I think. You're just greedy, money-motivated."
Salespeople think: "Clients are closed-minded."

Clients think: "You're cramming it down my throat."
Salespeople think: "Sales are appreciated. I'm doing this to help you. Now, have some pie."

This happens every day because, regardless of what side we are on—pro or con, home or away, salesman or customer—everyone thinks the other person has an agenda even though most of us are not subversive and only have the very best intentions. We have taken the way of the wild and made it the way of the world.

Salespeople attack with, "I'm only trying to help you and close the deal."

Clients become defensive and wonder, "How much are you going to make on me?"

The Kitchen Table

Joe scheduled an appointment with Byer B. Weyer from his cold-call list. He arrives at the Weyer residence and Byer invites him into the kitchen where they can get away from the noise. Joe has a strong handshake and a friendly smile. He compliments Byer's home. This all makes Byer feel good. He starts feeling really good…until he realizes that there is something to be sold, and unless he does something quick, he will be the one doing the buying! The defenses go up. Byer, the customer, becomes very cautious and begins to try to interpret the intentions of Joe, the salesperson. The salesperson notices less enthusiasm on the part of the customer and tries to involve the client in more conversation, trying to figure out the customer's needs. The customer feels like he is being interviewed, and is hesitant to reveal information, his interest, or his feelings. Without the right information, the salesperson tries to guess his "hot button" and resorts to pitching the product, the service, or the opportunity. Both customer and salesperson have set up camp at opposite sides of the kitchen table, and in between is a chasm of doubt. The customer doubts the sincerity of the representative and the product or service. The customer wonders about the commission and the salesperson's motive. He worries about being sold something that doesn't meet his needs, or making a mistake, or paying too much. The salesperson worries about the presentation, about closing the sale, about losing the sale.

Nowhere is the need for listening and trust more evident then in the sales process. People want to do business with people they can trust. They are afraid of being taken advantage of, of making a mistake, and of being "sold." Many times the customer does not trust the salesperson. Sometimes the salesperson does not trust the customer!

If we think about our own experiences as customers in the sales process we have often felt that salespeople are out for themselves, want to make a quick buck, aren't listening, and just don't understand us or our needs. The assumption is that the salesperson is only thinking of himself, his commission, his products, and his company, not us. There are times that concern is legitimate.

As salespeople working with customers, we may have felt that the customer was not listening, did not provide the right information, and didn't trust us. It can be uncomfortable on either side of the table, and because we have been on both sides of the table, we have a great opportunity in understanding our customers. We know that they have concerns about the process and about us. The best way to address these fears is by first understanding they do exist, and then demonstrate our concern for the customer by really listening. We all want to be trusted. It is hard to imagine that others might not trust us, but that is the truth. When we really listen, we allow others to share their concerns and can really begin to help them. It is amazing to see the receptiveness of others when we have first done the work of paying attention.

To achieve this receptiveness requires more than just knowing how to listen, it requires wanting to listen, really wanting to help. We have to be confident enough to listen first before moving into our pitch. The longer we listen, the more we understand what is important to the other. We must discover what the problems are if we are to help. What is the pain that they want to avoid, or the potential gain that they hope for? We are often in a rush to tell our story, to talk about our company, our products, our opportunity, or our solutions. Whenever we speak, people are either agreeing or disagreeing with us. If we communicate our message too quickly or forcefully, we force them to choose a response.

The difference between a good salesperson and a great salesperson is speed. The *slower* the better. This is contrary to a lot of sales training which focuses on trial closes, winning small agreements, option of choice closes, and a thousand other techniques. Listening is not a technique. Listening is to the sales process what the wind is to sailing. It helps us get to where we want to go. The focus of most salespeople is on the delivery, the telling, and the selling. We may learn scripts, prepare presentations, and practice techniques. When we do this, we know our scripts but not our clients. We know our presentations, but not our audience.

We try to be the experts. This is good because customers want an expert, but again, an expert who understands. They want us to be an expert in them and their needs, not an expert in selling. There is at least one major problem with being an expert…We might not be! While we may know a lot about something, and even more than most, we can't know it all. Someone says, "I am an expert on me." Oh, Really? How many hairs are on your head? If we set out thinking we know it all, there are a lot of people who will be very happy to prove us wrong, including potential customers. In our desire to tell more, we may miss more. We miss opportunities to discover real needs and buying motives. Without the help of our clients, we are giving them something to choose, or not choose. If we tell a client something is good, they must take us at our word or not. If they just accept what we tell them, and it proves unsatisfactory, they will view it as our fault. If they are given the time to determine it is good, it must be true. Our goal is to have them partner with us in finding the solution.

For every action, there is an equal and opposite reaction. If you push, they'll push back. If you listen, they'll speak. Some relationships have to be adversarial. With team sports, one team has to win. One team has to lose. If one team takes time to closely observe, to listen to their opponents, they can learn from them what it will take to beat them.

The client-sales relationship may be seen as adversarial and perceived as hunter-prey. Though this may be a common perception, it is a common misconception. What does the client want? A good product at a good price. What does the salesman want? To make money. On the surface, this sounds adversarial and counter-productive. However, this is really a win-win situation. When you're dealing with an ethical salesperson and a client who really wants to help himself, maybe the client won't always buy the most expensive item, but he'll be more likely to come back for more or recommend the salesperson to others. Together, they can find an "exact" solution to fit the client's needs and still make the salesman money, whereby, neither of them must compromise.

THE EXACT SOLUTION?

Listening is to the sales process what the wind is to sailing. It helps us get to where we want to go.

—Lou Garcia

There are certain considerations to make when looking for a solution. A good salesperson wants to say, "The solution to the problem is…" But to say that without listening first means there are assumptions being made.

First, we're assuming that **there is a problem**. What the salesperson perceives as a problem may not be a problem for the client. "You don't have enough life insurance coverage."

"I'm not married. I don't have children. Why do I need to leave money behind?"

Next, we're assuming that **there is a solution**. Sometimes, stuff happens. It may have been avoidable, but what's done is done. It can't always be fixed or replaced. There are times when you just have to cut your losses, pick up the pieces, and move on.

Then, we're assuming that **we have the solution**. We must be careful here because if we have the solution, we're obviously better than you, smarter than you, or richer than you.

Furthermore, we're assuming that **they want a solution**. Why would anyone even think of that as being an assumption? Of course people want solutions to their problems. Why wouldn't someone want a solution? "If I do this, something else, something worse may happen. I'd rather leave well enough alone."

In addition, we're assuming that **there is only one solution**. "**The solution** to the problem is…" In the words of Mighty Mouse, "Here I come to save the day!" How lucky is it that the customer managed to find you, the person who had the only existing solution to the problem.

Still, there is the assumption that **they have only one problem**. "The solution to **the problem** is..." But it may not be the only problem, so the solution may not work. They may not even be aware that there are other problems, or that may be the only one that concerns them at the moment.

Lastly, we are assuming that **our solution will be less expensive or time-consuming** than their current problem. Perhaps someone has less than perfect vision. Yes, his eyesight can be corrected with lasik surgery, but that's expensive. Glasses work fine, and he likes the way he looks wearing them.

When all is said and done...or in this case, before anything is said and done, that's a lot of assumptions being made:

> There is a problem...
>
> There is a solution...
>
> We have the solution...
>
> They want a solution...
>
> There is only one solution...
>
> They have only one problem...and
>
> Our solution will be less expensive or time-consuming.

FROM THE INSIDE OUT

o o o o o o o o o o o o o o o o o o o o o o o o o o o o o o
The best script for listening…begins as a blank page.

—*Norm Merritt*

So, we have to learn to listen. We have to learn how to listen and how to show we are listening. This is the basis of a listening model that ranges from the **Inside** to the **Outside**.

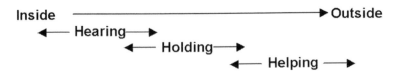

Hearing, **Holding**, and **Helping** are not independent steps that follow one after the next. They are three parts of the same process that build upon one another. Helping may start a little later into the conversation than the other two, but all three are interwoven throughout the conversation.

HEARING

○ ○
It is a rare person who wants to hear what he doesn't want to hear.

—Dick Cavett

A lot of ***hearing*** is done internally and is, therefore, not seen by the speaker. It is part of the preparation prior to and during the conversation. There are four factors of hearing to remember: Center, Clear, Check, and Create.

Center your attention. You really want to focus on the other person. Actually pay attention to the speaker. You can do this by maintaining eye contact. That doesn't mean to stare him down and never blink, but you should put some mental blinders on so that you're not looking in every direction every time something comes into your peripheral view. Eye contact doesn't necessarily mean looking directly into the eyes either, but you should remain somewhere on the speaker's face. Some people actually hear others better if they watch their lips while speaking. They're not reading their lips, but there is an association of movement with the sound. It demonstrates that they are paying attention.

Clear your mind. In the words of En Vogue, a popular 90's R&B group, "Free your mind…and the rest will follow." Yes, there are a lot of things going on in your life. Some of those things are good. Some may not be so good. There are always things to do, always places to be, always people to meet. Things have happened. Things will happen. Those are all the past and the future. You need to be in the moment for the moment because when the moment is gone, you can't get it back. To truly listen to someone else, you cannot allow yourself to be so self-absorbed and close-minded. If you lose the moment, you may lose the customer or the discussion.

Check your actions and reactions. Internally, you need to monitor yourself. As with driving, you have to concentrate on the road. When you find yourself drifting, you compensate by turning the steering wheel to get yourself back on course. Every so often, ask yourself if you're still listening. If you're not, steer yourself back to the speaker. Don't try to reconstruct what you may have missed because while you're reconstructing, you're not listening again and missing more. Just like driving, you have a destination you're trying to reach—making a point, closing a sale. At times, to reach your destination, you may need to steer yourself back on course. So, don't have other things in your hands either unless they are pertinent to the conversation such as pen and paper for taking notes. If you use a pen, don't sit there clicking it open and shut or fumbling around with it because that only serves as a distraction.

Create the best possible surroundings. You need to create an environment that limits interruptions. Turn off your cell phone. If your phone rings and you don't answer it, it is an annoying distraction. If you take a call, you make the phone call more important that the person you are with. Let the others know you are turning off the phone. It shows them you are courteous and sincere and that you are there for them. Leave your problems at the door, and whenever possible, shut the door. It keeps your problems and other distractions from popping in.

German theologian Paul Tillich stated: *The first duty of love is to listen.* Listening is really the greatest gift you can give. Give time to listen and focus on the speaker. Find out what you can learn from the conversation. Always be in the here and now, not the past or the future or thinking about another place. Find out what is important to you, what is important to them.

HOLDING

○ ○
One of the most valuable things we can do to heal one another is listen to each other's stories.

—Rebecca Falls

Part of finding out what is important to the other party is **holding**, learning and retaining information about the other person. This is partially invisible and part of what will be seen as you are obtaining information. How does holding work? First, be open-minded. You have to be open-minded if you ever expect to understand someone. One of our greatest internal barriers that prevent us from listening is that the majority of us are somewhat close-minded. We use much of our energy evaluating what others say then judging them based on our experiences. When we judge them, we are more prone to be selective in our listening and hear only what we want to hear, blocking out anything we judge as wrong.

Why do we spend so much time evaluating and judging others? We were raised that way. We begin making evaluations and judgments from the first day we learn. If I cry because I'm hungry and then get fed, then I should cry anytime I want anything so that I get what I want. Later I learn that crying won't get me everything, so I must beg. Later, begging doesn't work, so I have to take. Taking doesn't work, so I have to earn. As we grow, we are constantly learning and changing. We file this knowledge away in a mental filing cabinet for quick reference later in life. If we are not objective, we try to use these experiences to explain what others say, do, and need.

Joe has two children. Jose, named after him and his mother's father, and Maria. He was spending some quality time with Jose after his nap. Joe held up one ball and asked, "What color is this?"

Jose grabs at Joe's glasses. He calls out, "Blue!" or a reasonable facsimile.

"Blue! Right! My boy's a genius. One year old and he already knows his colors." Joe holds up another ball, a red one this time. "What color is this?"

"Blue!"

Joe shrugs. "Oh well." Jose is just starting to learn new words. Blue is what he knows, so everything is blue to him. "Let's go have some pie."

Maria is 4. He holds up the first ball for her. "What color is this?"

She chimes in, "Blue."

"En Español?"

"Azul." Maria is learning colors and languages. She knows exactly what blue is…for the moment. When she grows up, she'll no longer know "Blue." She'll start collecting these things called…shoes. Everything will change. Blue will no longer exist. Suddenly, there will be Navy Blue, Royal Blue, Midnight Blue, Sky Blue, Blue Sky (Believe it or not, that's two different colors. Really!), Powder Blue, Ocean Blue, Baby Blue…Blue Blue…

What happens to her mental filing cabinet? It expands. Next it happens with Greens. Then the Reds. Everything is connected. We continue to grow mentally, or we at least have the ability to. We learn. We change our way of thinking.

But at some point, we think our filing cabinets are filled to over-flowing, and we become set in our ways with an aversion to learning anything that might be contradictory. We no longer have room for anything else. Besides, what else is there? We think we know it all. Actually, we do know it all…about our own world. We know what we like and what we don't like. We know what we think is right or wrong. If we don't like it, then we start rejecting it. We start tearing down what they say before we try to understand why they are saying it. The problem is that we don't know what we don't know. We are secure in the knowledge of what we do know. The danger of listening to what we don't like is that we might have to change. What if, by some stretch of the imagination, someone else is right?

Understanding someone's motivation does not require that we have to accept that motivation and change our belief system. Don't just shake your head at someone to move the conversation along. And, by all means, don't just say, "I agree," because that will only result in a false sense of security and will eventually undermine their faith in you. When you allow yourself to undermine your character, things like competence will also come under fire. In the end, you may agree to disagree. This is fine when it is done with respect instead of ignorance and accusation. This is part of understanding the people with whom you speak. If you disagree with someone, you can leave or accept it…which means you might have to change.

If you're not open to change or listening to others, you become so set in your ways that you can't discern that what is right for one may not be right for all.

That afternoon, Joe and Martha left the kids with their grandmother to enjoy a quiet visit to the local museum. There was quite a good collection of art throughout history and a special show comparing the styles through time. In that one show, they saw how a variety of artists portrayed the same scene. The styles were widely varied:

Abstract	Art Deco
Caricature	Cubism
Dada	Expressionism
Functionalism	Impressionism
Mannerism	Modern
Neoclassical	Pointillism
Post-Impressionism	Primitive
Realism	Romanticism
Surrealism	Symbolism

In each case, though the subject was the same, the results were very different. Seen independently of one another, no one would have any idea that the paintings were related.

Leaving that room, they moved into the 20th century. The two disagreed on practically every piece of abstract art there. Joe would like what Martha didn't or vice versa. Neither of them saw the same thing when they looked at a particular piece. They did agree to disagree on what the artists' perceptions were based on the names of the paintings. They left the museum without knowing how they felt about most of what they saw.

Such variety is based on the fact that people see things in different ways. Their perceptions are based on their experiences, their moods, or their mental states at any given time. In 1921 Psychiatrist Hermann Rorschach even developed a psychiatric test based on such perceptions. Most people know this as inkblot tests. A person holds up a piece of paper with an abstract black design on it and asks the other person for the images and feelings inspired by the design. The results can be as diverse as the people taking the test.

People don't always see things the same way. People have different goals. People do what they do with different motivations. Even if they do the same things, it may be for different reasons.

If you're not open to the fact that different people have different needs, then you won't listen to them to find those needs. Instead, you'll find you lost the client. If you don't listen to their reasons and arguments, then you can't respond in a way to get your point across successfully. For us to be successful, we have to learn how to get in the other's world. It's our job to see what they want, what they need, what they believe, what their motivation is.

After we set the environment so that they will talk by making it clear that we will listen, the next thing we do behind the scenes is think about what they say. Thinking does not mean judging. Distance yourself to be more objective. It may sometimes be difficult to be objective because you are passionate about what you do and believe. Being objective means taking your emotions out of the thought process to gain a better understanding of the facts or of the other person's emotional and mental states. For the moment, it is about the other person. Don't rush through the yellow light. Seek to find out the reasons and emotions behind his actions, his thoughts and, sometimes, his fears. Don't make the king cut off your head. Find out what they are saying and why. To find out, you often need to ask questions.

Think back to the conversation Joe had with Miss Treetid.
...On the elevator, he ran into his acquaintance Miss Treetid. There was no one else in the elevator with them. "You know, Joe...It's this job." That's all she said, expecting Joe to rush into one of his tirades.
Joe chimed in when he realized the chance here. "My company..." He stopped himself. "What is it about your job?"
Miss Treetid would have stepped back, impressed by this show of concern, but she was already leaning against the elevator. "It's going nowhere. They don't treat me well."
"How long have you felt this way?"
"A while."
"Why haven't you done something about it?"
"The job market's not that great right now."

Joe is gathering information to learn more about her and how to help her. "Besides that, is there anything else bothering you?"

"Yeah. They haven't given me a raise in a year."

"Is that a problem?"

"Sure it is. I've run myself ragged for them."

"Do you think you'll get one next year?"

"Probably not…" The elevator reached her floor, and the door opened.

"Maybe we can talk more about this later."

"Maybe."

When we ask questions, people like us for caring. So we ask more questions. The more they like us, the more they trust us and the better our chances of closing the deal.

But we need to know when not to ask too many questions. There is a fine line between asking questions to learn more and the perception that we are being pushy and nosey. Silence can be equally valuable and important. There will be more on this later.

As we listen, it may help to jump into the conversation as long as we can do it without interrupting. Entering the conversation at this point is not to give a solution but to clarify what we have heard. You can lead into it with lines like: "Is what you're saying…" "What I'm hearing is…" "Do I understand correctly that…" Don't repeat them word for word. That will sound as though you are only spouting off what you have heard. They'll answer with a "Yes" because if this is done verbatim, how can they disagree? It will show that you were listening, not that you were gaining an understanding. When they say "Yes" like that, they may get a false sense of satisfaction for a time, and you'll think you are happier because they are agreeing with you. Paraphrase whenever possible. By rephrasing what they said, they feel understood, and you actually understand. If you don't understand correctly, it gives them the opportunity to correct what they said or what you heard.

Not everything needs to be repeated. It's up to you to know when clarification isn't needed. If someone tells you, "My name is Bob," it shouldn't be necessary to say, "So, what you're saying is…your name is Bob."

Before moving on to Helping, let's take a moment to consider motives and techniques.

Modus Operandi

These processes, Hearing and Holding, are some of the techniques needed to become a successful listener. Since some of the actions involved are visible, they are very important to master.

> **technique** *n:*
>
> 1: an art or practical method applied to a particular task
>
> **2: a skillful command of fundamentals derived from practice and familiarity;** "practice greatly improves proficiency"

Techniques are very superficial, the face of your motives, the reflection of your motives. People recognize techniques, and your techniques can break a sale and cause someone to lose interest in you. Techniques have to be practiced and honed. They are **how** you do what you do.

The best way to improve your techniques is to focus on your motives. These motives are your driving force. They are **why** you do what you do. While techniques are important to help the process and learn necessary information, you must be backed up with a desire to help others find the right solution. If your motives are weak, your techniques will reflect that weakness as you simply go through the motions. People will see that weakness because you will come across as insincere. Sincerity is one of your best tools for getting from motives (why) to techniques (how). If you have faith in what you do, if you believe in your product, your techniques will be directly influenced and sincere.

People are even characterized by their techniques. Just like hair color, eye color, height, weight, and tattoos, their techniques can identify the person. Police agencies establish a *modus operandi* (method of operation) for a suspect based upon previous actions. By recognizing techniques they can try to predict a suspect's next move or even attribute an event to a particular person. What you do is by no means criminal, but your method of operation can give you away and cost you. Your techniques will most likely give you away if you don't have good motives behind them. You do not want your modus operandi to identify you to your clients strictly as a *salesperson*. More importantly than practicing your techniques is ensuring that your motives are sincere. You are there to do more than make a sell to your clients. You are there to offer them assistance, to better their lives. Why do you want to **help them**? What is it you are trying to **do for them**? What do you want to **offer them**? With sincere motives, your techniques will reflect those motives to make it less likely that you will lose out.

You may have been taught the technique of using feel, felt, found. It goes like this:

> I know how you **feel**…
>
> At first, I **felt** this option was too expensive…
>
> What I **found** was that option was the best bet for my money…

Though this technique implies empathy, it has drawbacks. When listening to someone express his feelings, be careful not to jump on board with him too quickly. "I know how you feel." Do you? You actually don't. You may have an idea about his feelings, but you don't really know because you are not him, you have not lived his life or gone through the identical experiences. "What you feel is…" That's wrong. With this, you are in effect telling him how he feels rather than your perception of his feelings. This is especially bad if you haven't taken the time to get to know them. If you have listened, they may be more willing to forgive you, chalking it up to a bad choice of words.

"I felt the same…" Wrong! "I" implies that infinite wisdom. Do you really know how everyone else feels? Is your marriage unhappy? Did you come from a broken home? Did your mother die when you were young? There are an infinite number of possibilities why someone feels a particular way.

"What I found was…" Wrong again! "I" implies that you have the solution. It says that you know more than the other person. What worked for you may not work for another for as many reasons as why someone feels a particular way.

Watch your technique. Watch your body language. If it's too animated, people can tell you're not listening. Watch your tone when responding. Distance and disinterest are easily revealed in your sound even if not in your words. Pretend listening makes someone feel worse then crummy because it's sarcastic and patronizing.

A Note on Technique—Norm Merritt

> This may sound cliché, but after a few hours of writing this the other day, I was on the phone with a friend (no name used to protect him). He uses a hands-free headset on his cordless phone so he can move around his house and work on chores while we talk. He prides himself on his ability to multi-task. As I talked and he listened, he responded at the right places. Then his responses became slightly delayed. I supposed he was taking time to process what I said. It wasn't a heart-to-heart, so nothing was too deep to require

much processing. His tone gradually changed. "Yep." "Yeah." "Uh huh." "Uh...huh." "...Uh.........huh." So I told him I was pregnant. His response was a delayed "Uh...huh." We *talked* for a few more minutes before I had to laugh. Saying I was pregnant wouldn't have been such a big deal except that...I'm a man. His technique was poor, and I caught him on it. In this case, there was no harm done. We're good friends who are there for one another. Despite the poor technique, I knew his motives were sincere.

Focus on your motives. Why are you engaged in this conversation in the first place? You want to make your sale...to make your point. If you want it to work, you need to overcome whatever obstacles there are to be open-minded and listen. What are you providing, serving, teaching, or helping your clients with? Connect to the possibilities you are creating for your clients. How will they benefit? How will they feel? Make sure your motives are not strictly self-serving. If they are, you won't care what the other person is saying, and your techniques will give you away.

Other possible obstacles that you need to look out for are laziness and boredom. Both of these can keep you from giving proper attention to the other party. It takes work to be attentive when you have other things on your mind. It takes even more work if you have limited interests or are not interested in what you are doing.

A Note on Motives—Lou Garcia

At 21, my interest was girls. I didn't even have interests. Only interest. Girls. Some of my friends were interested in their cars. Me...only girls. Some of my friends had gotten married and had kids. Me...only girls. There were times when I thought all they ever wanted to talk about was their children.

Children weren't on my radar. They weren't a part of my world. I would always say, "Yeah. Uh-huh. Really?" Then I would flash a smile to my waitress. Pretend listening. They would show me baby pictures from the nursery hours after the delivery. They looked like...I didn't know...all red and winkled, like some alien.

But the minute I had children, my world changed. Now, I was the one with all the pictures to show. I'm sure that I lost some friends back then because of my inability to show genuine interest in their lives. If I had done more to move into their world, what would it be like today? I might still have them as friends. If I had spent more time understanding them and their concerns as parents, could I have become a better parent myself?

Just remember that you can change and adapt to new interests and new situations. Think back to the cars you have bought over the years. There are some cars I never really noticed. When the time came to buy a new car, I bought a Mustang because it was one of the first cars I looked at, and I don't like to shop. It was a perfectly good car, but it wasn't my dream car. Just days after I drove it off the lot, everywhere I looked, I saw Mustangs. I never recalled seeing that many before. With the purchase of that car, my world had changed.

So, how are we supposed to improve our techniques to properly reflect our motives? How do we narrow our focus while expanding our horizons? If we don't know what we don't know, how can we improve our ability to listen? We do so by listening and learning. Our listening gets better if we practice our listening. The more we listen, the more we learn. The more we learn, the more we understand. The more we understand, the more they feel understood. The more they feel understood, the more they are willing to open up. The more they open up to us, the more open they will be to us. Point made. Sale closed. Game. Set. Match.

As we listen to learn, we learn to listen. As with anything, listening takes practice. Some say, "Practice makes perfect." Vince Lombardi said: "Practice doesn't make perfect. Perfect practice makes perfect." However, everyone can improve. Perfection is a goal but can be unsettling to some because it is unattainable. They get scared and stop. The Germans have a similar saying: *Übungen macht der Meister*. This means: *Practice makes the master*. It doesn't require perfection, just practice. There are certain things we can all do while we listen to make us listen better.

Look for areas of agreement.
Check for completion.
Look for feeling.
Watch for consistency.
Ask questions.
Internally summarize.

Look for areas of agreement. This can be a cultural challenge to overcome. In the West, people are very competitive. When two people have two differing ideas, the tendency is to fight it out. There is no gray area. If the ideas are different, one must be wrong, and the other must be right. I would never have a wrong idea, so you can't be right, and you need to change…period.

This isn't to say there are no disagreements in Eastern society. But in the East, they approach differences by looking for areas of agreement. By knowing what they agree on, they are more likely able to determine at what point they disagree and why. This constructs a foundation on which they can build.

Many families need financial advice. Helping families is good. Everyone can agree on that. We may disagree about life insurance, investing, or the stock market. But at least we can start with the agreement that helping them is good and then determine the best course of action.

The customer is always right. That's what the customer thinks.

The customer doesn't know what he wants. That's what the salesperson thinks.

This sets up the scene for disagreement. What they both must realize is that the customer has come to the salesperson for a reason. They can start with the agreement that the customer has a need. They can build on that agreement. They can define the need and work towards a solution together. When the salesperson comes to the client, they can both agree that the salesperson has something to offer. From there, they can see if what is offered will fit an existing need.

Look for completion. When listening to someone, just because he finishes a sentence, he may not be finished with a thought. A pause doesn't mean it's time to interject. Interrupting doesn't happen only in the middle of a sentence. It can happen in the middle of a thought in a moment of silence. The other person may be thinking about what to say next. Make sure he is done. Don't say anything at first. Osmosis can be a useful principle to fill the silence.

> **os·mo·sis** (ŏz-mō'sĭs) *n.*
>
> **...2. A gradual and often unconscious process of assimilation or absorption:** *learned German by osmosis while living in Munich for 15 years.*

Okay, maybe that's not too clear, or it's a little too scientific for here. To paraphrase, things move from areas of higher concentration to areas of lower concentration. If you keep silent for a moment, sound will tend fill the silence. There is a pretty good chance that the other person will start talking, providing you with still more information.

If necessary, ask questions to check for completion. Some possible examples are:

> *"Besides that, what else is bothering you?"*
>
> *"If I could help you with that, would that solve all your problems?"*
>
> *"Is there anything else that you feel is important?"*

Look for feeling. People get emotional when they talk. When they are encouraged to talk and allowed to speak freely, they tend to let their emotions show. When they feel threatened, they will mask their emotions in order to protect themselves. Some people are guarded all the time. The best way to read someone's emotional state is to get to know him. The best way to do that is by listening. Once again, you have to listen in order to learn to listen.

Sometimes, we ask questions the wrong way. If someone has strong feelings about a subject and we ask questions, they may become defensive. Any salesperson knows that money is an emotional subject. It isn't the numbers themselves, but the situations around it. If the client was talking about his bills the night before and how no matter what he did he didn't think he could ever get out of debt and that it was his fault for letting things get out of hand, asking him questions about his finances may strike a nerve with him. He will feel pressured and insecure. If you ask too quickly, he'll feel pushed and will push back.

In actuality, you are sincerely trying to understand him by asking questions. But if he is in no mood for questions, he will feel that you are interrogating him. Anyone with teenage children knows how difficult it can be to find out anything about them. Ask one question, and they feel like you're giving them the third degree. Some people call this probing, but how many people ever tell you to "Stop probing me!"?

Joe has been married for seven years. He sometimes feels his wife is interrogating him. When he comes home after a tough day, Martha asks, "Baby, what's wrong?"

Joe says, "Nothing."

When he says "Nothing," what does he mean? When most men say "Nothing," what do they mean? Nothing? Pretty much. They mean they don't want to talk about it.

When Joe comes home and sees that Martha has had a bad day, he asks, "Baby, what's wrong?"

She says, "Nothing."

Joe knows how he feels when he says the same thing, so he says, "OK," and walks away.

Suddenly, he's in so much trouble. Does "Nothing" mean "Nothing" for her? NO!

Does "Nothing" mean "I don't want to talk about it?" NO!

"Nothing" means "Something. If you love me, you'll stop and ask." After seven years, you would expect Joe to know this.

Look at many couples that have been married for so many years. This still happens to them as they fail to be objective. After so long, they think they're so much alike and attune to the other person that they are bound to feel the same way and communicate the same way. They may deny it, but if you ask any of their children…"Oh boy…"

Back to when Joe told Martha, "Nothing…"
Martha asks, "Is it work?"
"It's nothing."
"Is it the house?"
"No. It's nothing."
"Is it me? It's not work. It's not the house. It must be our relationship."
"No!" Now, Joe is snippy. What he needs is to go into his private space, back to his solitary roots, his cave. All he has to do is disappear for a while. A little later, he'll come out, and he'll be fine.

But Martha follows him to his cave because she wants to help. She steps inside and asks, "Is it…"

Never! Ever! Never go into Joe's cave! Get out!

Martha's not being mean. Her motives aren't to interrogate Joe. It's her way of caring. She believes that Joe's "Nothing" means "Something, and if you love me, you'll ask." When he said, "Nothing," she heard "Something," so she asks more questions.

Part of the responsibility of any relationship is to understand the other person. There is so much more than the words when a conversation is taking place. Along with the verbal are the mental, the emotional, and the physical. It's the words, the motivation, the feelings, and the body language. It makes no difference whether it is a personal or a professional relationship. If someone doesn't want to speak, then listening is not an option.

So, Joe leaves the house for a while and goes over to Bart's place. "Man, I've had a rough day."
"Great! Let's have a beer," or "Let's go jogging."
What Joe wants is relaxation, a distraction, or a drink. He doesn't want to talk about it. He doesn't want to think about it. Thinking about it only makes him feel worse. He feels like Martha is trying to give him the third degree.

You have to know when and when not to ask questions. That requires objectivity and familiarity.

Now, what about when Martha had a bad day? Being the salesman that he is, he thinks he knows everything. What Martha needed was a little advice. Joe fixes things…situations…the car…the lawn mower…her. It's all the same to him. So, he starts fixing her…advising her on what she should do.

Back when they first started dating, she would listen to his advice and humor him with: "Oh, you're so smart." "You're so nice." "You're so intelligent." Once they were married, she would be able to train him. When Joe heard: "Oh, you're so smart." "You're so nice." "You're so intelligent," he heard that he was smart, nice, and intelligent, so he must have been doing things right.

Martha didn't want advice from him. She wanted to talk and have him listen. She wanted to talk about her day while talking about Joe's day was the last thing he wanted to do.

Men speak an average of 6000 words a day. Women, on the other hand, speak on the average 18,000 words a day. That's 12,000 words more.

By the time Joe gets home after being at work all day, he ran out of his 6000 words around 3:35pm. He pushed it further with his 4:00pm conference call. He's done for the day.

After being at home with the kids, Martha still has 14,423 to go. She's still in her pajamas. Her hair's messed up. Her coffee's cold. She wants to talk.

Instead of listening, Joe gives her advice. "Read a book." "Go to a seminar." "Take a run."

"Run? Are you saying I need to lose weight? You're saying I'm fat!"

"No, I'm not. You're not listening." But Joe's in trouble again. He said to go running because it's the kind of thing he would do to feel better. "How about some pie?"

Next door, there were times when Bart's wife, Stacey, would come home after a long and slow day. "I hate my job."

"Then quit," is Bart's advice to her.

Stacey says sarcastically, "Oh, that never occurred to me. That's why I married you…Mighty Mouse." *Here I come to save the day!*

Bart tries to console her. "No. You're not listening."

"Of course I am."

"But you don't understand."

"So, you're saying I'm stupid."

Stacey would come home another time. "My boss is a jerk."

Bart tells her again, "Then quit."

She says sarcastically: "Oh, that never occurred to me. That's why I married you...Mighty Mouse." *Here I come to save the day!*

He says, "No. You're not listening."

"Of course I am."

He says, "You don't understand."

"So, you're saying I'm stupid."

The next week when Stacey came home, she starts with, "Those people at work make me crazy."

"Then quit."

"Oh, that never occurred to me. That's why I married you...Mighty Mouse." *Here I come to save the day!*

"No. You're not listening."

"Of course I am."

"You don't understand."

"So, you're saying I'm stupid." Bart is obsessing about the situation now because Stacey isn't taking his advice.

"No, dear. Have some pie."

Giving unsolicited advice only increases the distance between two parties. Try helping someone who doesn't want help. It isn't easy and can do more harm than good. Giving advice makes everything sound so easy that the other person loses self-confidence. The other person may begin to wonder, "What's wrong with me? Why couldn't I come up with that myself?"

Joe and Martha and Brad and Stacey were driven by their love for one another, their desire to fix each other. Love is good, but not necessarily the best driver. Sometimes, a little objectivity is needed. In the business world, the relationships aren't as intimate, but for a good professional relationship, concern for one another is still there. You should always strive to be objective. Try to understand a person's emotional state when engaged in a conversation. It's very difficult to judge someone's emotional state when your emotions get in the way. If they appear agitated, slow down. Don't rush the yellow light. When they become evasive, hesitant, fidgety, they may be trying to avoid a collision. When their lips tighten or their voice cracks, you should hit the brakes before they hit you.

History has conditioned man to provide. For centuries, he would bring home the meat. The woman would realize, "Wow! You did something." Today, both the man and the woman provide for the family. So the man must find another way to feel useful. He does this by giving advice. It's his way of fixing things. He is doing something. When two men are involved, they'll both try to fix things, each thinking he can do a better job. Two women will be more likely to communicate before trying to fix anything.

Joe works in an office building in Atlanta. His wife Martha works at home. They live in a sub-division with 59 houses. Out of those, maybe 3 people are home during the day. Martha has no network any longer. There are no clotheslines or bridge clubs like a few decades ago. Martha calls her sister in Phoenix every day so she can talk to someone in order to use up some of her 18,000 daily words.

One way Joe can provide for her is by providing her with his attention and time to listen. So, he goes to the freezer and pulls out the Godiva ice cream. Then he gets spoons for everyone, and they all sit around the table. His job is to keep his mouth full of ice cream so that when she says something, all he can say is "Mmmm." This took him a long time to learn because he thought listening was too passive. He doesn't want to be passive. He wants to act. He needs to score points for what he does.

Men think we get points for doing stuff. We live our lives on a 1-to-1 scale for those points. Eye for eye. Tit for tat. However, women were simultaneously raised on a different scale. But no one thought about communicating this fact to the men. John Gray, author of *"Men are from Mars; Women are from Venus,"* helped to clarify this point system for all to understand.

Men: When we give our wives $100, we think we earn 100 points.
Women: When our husbands give us $100, they earn 1 point.

Men: When we give our wives $300, we think we earn 300 points.
Women: When our husbands give us $300, they earn 1 point.

Men: $60 for a dozen roses is 60 points. Even at her stingiest, it's a dozen roses, so it's 12 points.
Women: A dozen roses means 1 point.

So, men invented giving two-dozen roses on Valentine's Day because they think it doubles the points.

Women: 1 point.

Women: A trip to Hawaii, dinner, and dancing...1 point.

Men: $300, two-dozen roses, a trip to Hawaii, dinner, and dancing..."Please...2 points!"

Women: "Ha! 1 point."

Men begin to think that no matter what they do, they can't get ahead. If that's how it's going to be, why should they do anything? But all is not lost.

Listen to her completely for 1 full sentence and thought.

Men: 0 points

Women: 1 Point. For every sentence, she gives a point. Soon, men are racking the points up.

When Joe is speaking, he goes:

"Blah blah blah...period." Point made.

When it's Martha's turn, it's:

"Blah, blah, blah...comma..."

"Blah, blah, blah...comma..."

"Blah, blah, blah...comma..."and finally,

"Blah, blah, blah...semicolon."

"Blah, blah, blah...comma..."

"Blah, blah, blah...comma..."

"Blah, blah, blah...comma..."

"Blah, blah, blah...point."

When she gets to her point, he gets a point. How hard was that. Like Paul Tillich said: *The first duty of love is to listen.*

Sometimes, she'll try to trick him. She gets to a break and asks, "What do you think?"

Look out, Joe! That's a trick! If he answers immediately, he was evaluating and working through it all in his head, sidetracked into formulating his advice for her instead of listening. He was trying to do something. His answer should be delayed to make sure she has finished. He could always ask for more information, or if necessary, he can clarify.

Once again, it's the listener's job to create the right environment.

When Martha says, "I don't know why you married me," Joe should not take inventory and give her reasons. When she tells him, "The kids would be better off in an orphanage," Joe should not interject with reasons why that isn't so. Her statements were rhetorical. She isn't really looking for answers. She just wants to get her feelings out in the open. Joe needs to create an environment for listening to make her comfortable. If she is given the opportunity and feels free to speak, she can relax, relate, and release. In the end, she feels better, and Joe doesn't have to sleep on the sofa. For some, it's not the destination; it's the journey. This is the abstract art of conversation.

A conversation can be a lot like shopping. Martha loves to shop, but Joe hates it. When he goes to buy a shirt…he goes to buy a shirt. It's that easy. He buys a shirt. If it's on sale…he buys two. Can it get any easier than that?

On the other hand, Martha goes to buy a dress. She looks around through all the racks with Joe tagging along. She never picks the slinky, low-cut, slit-legged ones that he likes. She eventually picks out a navy blue one, hands Joe her purse, and he takes a seat in the solitary man-chair you always find outside the dressing room almost beneath a clothes rack. And there is the inevitable sleeve that hangs a little too low, brushing against his ear each time he moves. She disappears for several minutes into a world unknown to men.

Eventually, she comes out. "What do you think?"

Joe pushes the sleeve aside. He stands, purse in hand. "Great. Let's go."

"I don't know." She frowns. "It doesn't look quite right on me." She runs to the rack in her stocking feet and pulls out a Midnight Blue dress then disappears again.

Joe lost his seat to another husband who wanted to be somewhere else. He tries to hide Martha's purse behind him. A little later, she comes back out, "How's this one?"

"Great. Let's go."

She looks at the tag and frowns, a frown just slightly different than the other one. "I don't want to spend this much."

"Don't worry about the money. We can…" As she tiptoed over to select a Dark Blue dress, Joe grabbed the man-chair when the other one had stood to look at his wife.

She disappeared into the great unknown again. After several minutes, she came out again. "How about this one?"

"Great! Perfect! Let's get all three. Let's go."

She spun around, picked the dress up a bit then let it fall. She paused and pondered then looked over her shoulder and down. "Does this make me look fat?"

"No! You've got a beautiful body."

There is a slight hesitation before she flashes him a smile then returns into the dressing room one last time.

"Thank goodness it's over. She'll get that one."

She came out several moments later. "I can't find anything."

"WHAT! What about those three?" If Joe goes to buy a shirt and doesn't get one, he's ticked!

Martha smiles and says, "That was fun," then skips off.

He follows her, still holding her purse, holding it out for her to take. "Fun? That was not fun! You did not accomplish the mission. You did not kill the animal! How was this fun!"

Trying it on. Trying it on. Trying it on. For her, it was the event, not the end.

This is very analogous to listening. Joe had a point to make. Buying the shirt was his mission. For Martha, her mission was the entire experience regardless of the outcome. It helps to know when someone's talking is the means to the end or when that means is the end. By knowing, you can listen accordingly and respond only when necessary.

Listening is needed for any relationship to work. What you learn in your professional life can be applied at home. What you learn at home carries over into your professional life. The dynamics may be different, but relationships are relationships. There are commonalities and differences, agreements and arguments, needs and solutions, and benefits to any of them. In any case, we must learn to listen. If we interrogate by asking an associate too many questions before he is emotionally ready, he won't talk. If we offer advice before our spouses are finished talking, they won't feel understood and will be less likely to accept the advice. If we tell a client the solution to a problem before we define his needs, our character and competence are called into question, and we won't make the sell.

Watch for consistency. Once again, communication is made up of more than words. It's the tone, the intent, and the expression. These will go hand in hand…in hand when the speaker is sincere. Tone can be calm, sarcastic, angry, or frustrated. The intent is the motivation, more difficult to detect and usually developed through the course of the conversation. The motivation may be to humor, frighten, inform, or mislead. The expression is the person's bearing—posture, gestures, attentiveness, or nervousness. If any of these do not mirror the vocalized words, that may be more than what is being said, or what is being said could be wrong. That doesn't mean the person is lying. Something said sarcastically could be a way of humorously expressing a truth or defensively making a point.

When someone tells you nothing is wrong, does his body language mirror the statement? Does he avoid looking you in the eye? Is he holding back some pertinent information? Be prepared to react and respond accordingly.

Internally summarize. During a pause, not while someone is speaking to you, ask yourself, "Do I understand this?" "Is this the complete story?" Remember not to do this while the person is talking, because at this point, you have stopped listening and started analyzing. Keep this internal, both vocally and expressively. Remain focused on the other person. Don't roll your eyes up in contemplation or mouth the question so the other person thinks something else may be going on.

Ask questions. If you don't understand, ask questions to see if what you think you heard makes sense. Make sure you have a good picture.

HELPING

o o o o o o o o o o o o o o o o o o o o o o o o o o o o o o
There is only one rule to become a good talker...learn how to listen.

—Unknown

You've worked on hearing the other person. Improved concentration prepares you to be in the moment, to make the other person a priority. It opens you up for input so you can learn about your client, associate, or spouse. You've worked on learning and holding onto the information. That allows you to translate and understand what people tell you. You can begin to formulate your plan of attack to suitably meet the needs of others. Now, you need to keep them talking. You need to maintain the environment that helps communication.

It is always important to encourage communication if you wish to learn. The golden rule of listening is: *Not just to listen unto others as you would have them listen unto you, but to listen unto others as they would like to be listened to.* Don't listen to others as you would have them listen to you. For whatever reason, some people want to be treated differently. Some may require more help than others. With good techniques, you can coax almost anyone into talking by sustaining a high comfort level. For many, there is no higher praise than someone saying, "You're so easy to talk to."

As with Hearing and Holding, Helping will only improve with practice. This isn't a script. These are only pointers to set you in the right direction.

Watch Body Language

Be aware that body language is a language all its own. Nothing else this silent could speak so loudly. It is more instinctual than the spoken word, so it is harder to control and conceal. As far as you are concerned when you are listening, you can nod if you are sincere. Your body will give you away if you are not listening.

Your eyes will glaze over. They may become transfixed if you are bored. They'll get wider as your mind travels somewhere else. You'll twitch when you realize that you've left the moment and pull yourself back. Try not to have pen or paper in your hand unless it is necessary. Little is more distracting to either party than one of you clicking a pen open and shut or spinning it around your fingers or the rustling of papers as you pretend to organize yourself. Nervousness like that declares that you have other things on your mind or that you would rather be somewhere else. If you exhibit any of these characteristics, you will put distance between you and the other person. A speaker will either become silent or find a reason to leave.

The same applies to the speaker. You cannot control his body language, but as you make him more comfortable, the body language will begin to speak the same language as his words. If he won't look you in the eye, there could be something he is concealing. If he is fidgeting, you may need to pull back and take it as a yellow light. You may have to stop and take the conversation down another road. The new route will take longer, but it's better than having a collision and never reaching your destination.

Help Communication

How can you practice helping others communicate?

Ask questions to learn. Ask questions to confirm. As long as someone isn't being evasive or defensive, questions are perfect for getting the other person to talk. The questions may be leading. As you listen and internally summarize during the silent moments, you will have a better idea what solution may work or in which direction you want to take the conversation. When you ask questions, the other person doesn't think you are trying to force a solution or idea on him. But the questions shouldn't begin with phrases like "Shouldn't you..." or "Don't you think you need..." These are indeed questions, but barely. You are actually projecting on him what you think he should do or think, in effect saying, "If I were you..." Remember, you are not the other person. The point of listening is to learn about him, to understand him, not to understand yourself.

Your questions should be objective...not subjective. *"How did that make you feel?" "How long have you felt this way?"* These are *feeling* questions designed to provide a better understanding of your clients without putting them on the defensive.

Maintain a positive attitude. Sometimes it may not be possible to be positive about a particular situation because the situation is not a matter of right or wrong but of upsetting events. But you can be positive in letting others know it is all right to share.

Don't judge. Telling people what they shouldn't do or what they shouldn't think is as bad as telling them what they should do or think. People become very offended when others say their beliefs are wrong. Other cultures and sub-cultures have different beliefs, and you should respect those beliefs even if you don't agree with them. When you judge, you're once again projecting yourself on them instead of learning about them. The end result is that you lose the client or the argument. If they feel free to communicate now, that opens them up now and later, and it encourages them to let others know they can talk with you without fear of reprisal.

Clarify. Ask them to clarify if necessary. It may not be possible for you to reiterate what you've been told. Maybe you did get inadvertently sidetracked and missed a detail or twelve. If you can't figure it out, the more they can develop their thoughts, the better you will understand. Clarifying as a means of helping follows the same rules as clarifying for holding.

Some questions you may ask to gain a clearer picture are:

> *Can you help me understand that?*
>
> *Can you show me how…?*
>
> *Am I correct in thinking…?*
>
> *Can you give me a little more detail?*

These questions give others the opportunity to provide you with more information about themselves and to correct anything they may have not made clear or that you may have heard incorrectly.

Get them involved in the solution. As you learn about them, they may be learning about themselves. The more they know about themselves, the more they can tell you about themselves. The more they can tell you, the more they can do to help themselves. Let them help you. People will be more than happy to help you understand them. It gives them a chance to fix things, making them feel useful in the process. They can become excited about helping, because they will get to share in the victory.

Be quiet. Select your words carefully and use them sparingly. The object here is to listen, learn then solve. Let them talk. Silence is golden, and that gold can line your pockets. Don't speak out of turn. Your chance will come soon enough, and you don't want to run out of your daily supply of words.

Improving Your Ability To Help

Take a deep breath. It keeps you from talking too soon. Also, breathing can keep you focused and in control of your emotional state. *In with the good air…Out with the bad.*

Consider your reputation with relationships, work, team members, and clients. The first impression is already made, but impressions can change. If you make a good first impression, it's easier to maintain, but don't think you can't make a bad second impression. Likewise, if you make a mistake at the beginning, don't give up and walk away. It may be harder to recover, but most people are willing to give someone a second chance.

Think of them. How are they going to feel when everything is done? If the intended result is to help them solve a problem, how should they feel when that problem is solved? What can you do to make sure they feel that way?

Eliminate distractions. If you have control over a possible distraction, do what you can to eliminate it. If they are in your office, close your door, ask not to be interrupted, have someone hold your calls. If you go to their home, turn off your cell phone. You're a little limited as to what you can do when you're in their environment. If you're in a public place, recommend a more isolated table away from most of the activity and put away your cell phone. If you bring someone into your home to talk, select a room where you are less likely to be disturbed. Keep away from the television, keep pets out of the room. Once again, turn off your phone. These days, phones are the most common distractions because we now have one with us everywhere we go. In our efforts to stay connected, we disconnect from the people we should be concentrating on, the people directly in front of us. When you interrupt someone to answer your phone, you are making the person on the phone more important and belittling the person you are with.

Imagine there will be a test afterwards. Would you have done things differently if there had been a test? Would you have concentrated more? Keep in mind that though you aren't being graded on this, you can still pass or fail. When everything is done, you have to decide if you did everything you could to make the meeting a success. Did you get the results you wanted? Did you learn about the other person? Did you convince the other person to buy your product or your side of the argument? Did you meet the client's needs in a fair and equitable way? **<u>Results are the bottom line.</u>**

WRAP UP

o o o o o o o o o o o o o o o o o o o o o o o o o o o o o o
No one ever listened himself out of a sale.

—Lou Garcia

Are you ready to rush out and listen? This certainly seems like a lot to remember when you're in a conversation. How can you expect to truly listen when you have to work so hard to keep yourself in check? You have to decide when it's appropriate to speak. You have to be careful about letting stray thoughts influence you. You have to keep control over your body. When you're trying to learn more about someone else, you must make yourself more objective and not be as influenced by your emotions as you are by their emotions. You're one person. How difficult it must seem to control your mouth, mind, body, and heart. But you're the only person who can. And you have as much to lose as the other person.

Don't think that you are responsible for the entire conversation and interaction. As important as listening is, you can't listen if the other person doesn't speak. He has a responsibility to say what he means, to be forthright and sincere. He shouldn't expect you to live by: *I know it's what I said, but it's not what I meant.* If he wants help, he has to be clear and concise. He must be willing to help because communication is a two-way street, but more importantly, your motives have to be right. However, you can't control him, nor should you want to. Since we are all individuals, you only have the ability to control yourself and must shape yourself accordingly. You must train yourself to control yourself because you are your greatest asset or liability. Which do you choose to be?

We live in a world of habits. Good ones and bad ones are developed early on in life. It takes time to break bad habits and to shape new ones. It takes practice. But always examine your motives. If your motives are sincere and you turn techniques into good habits, you will have better business, better sales, better recruits, and better relationships.

0-595-27453-6

Made in the USA
San Bernardino, CA
02 February 2014